For Arthur, Lucas, and one to come

Text and Images Copyright © by Little Stitches Books

No part of this book may be reproduced in any manner whatsoever without written permission except in the case of brief quotations embodied in critical articles and reviews.

Be the first to hear about new releases and join the Mailing list at LittleStitchesBooks.com

----
ISBN: 978-1-0692837-3-3

First Edition

Welcome friends!

Welcome friends, come join the show,
Dinos dance, and lights will glow!

Step inside, the beat is tight,
Let's boogie and groove on through the night!

Tyrannosaurus Rex

T. Rex stomps with his mighty feet,
Short arms bounce to the disco beat!

Volcano glows, a fiery sight,
Keep on dancing through the lava light!

Pterodactyl

Gliding high, and spinning around,
Leather wings flash, up and down!

Clouds drift by as the disco shines,
Soaring up on those funky lines!

Megalodon

Sharky spins and flips with flair,
Purple lights shining down everywhere!

Coral sways, in neon blue,
Megalodon sharks can boogie too!

Spinosaurus

Spino sways with flashing lights,
Grooves and glows on disco nights!

Armored sail, and stomping feet,
Dancing wild to the dinosaur beat!

Brontosaurus

Bronto bops, so tall and proud,
Neck sways gently going through the crowd.

Jungle beats, and stomping fun,
Dancing until the night is done!

Ankylosaurus

Anky grins and shakes his tail,
Multicolored lights while music wails!

Armored tough, but light on feet,
Rockin' on down to that funky beat!

Triceratops

Triceratops twirls, so full of grace,
Butterflies dancing all over the place!

Pebbles crunch, beneath each spin,
Smiling wide, let's jiggy again!

Iguanodon

Iguanodon stands so strong and tall,
Lava glows bright, beneath it all.

Spotlights shine, and light the way,
Serious moves on full display!

Stegosaurus

Stego stomps, his plates aglow,
Volcano sparks a fiery show!

Disco ball spins round up so high,
Shuffle on down under a starlit sky!

Velociraptor

Raptor jumps up, and spins around,
Tapping his claws, upon the ground!

String lights twinkle, palms sway too,
Twisting on down to the disco crew!

Thanks for coming!

The disco fades, the stars shine bright,
Our dinos danced, with all their might!

Thanks for coming, one last cheer,
Let's do it again, same time next year!

www.ingramcontent.com/pod-product-compliance
Lightning Source LLC
Chambersburg PA
CBHW041440010526
44118CB00002B/137